I write this book as an invocation to God. I have heard and thought so much about Him; have put aside other relationships in order to find out who He is. I am fascinated by His intricacy, His brilliance and yet His eternal gentleness.

Anthea Church

INVOCATIONS

ISBN 1-886872-03-1

Author - Anthea Church

Published by Brahma Kumaris Information Services
Global Co-operation House
65 Pound Lane, London NW10 2HH UK

First Edition Printed January 1997
by Leighton Printing Company, London, UK

This book has been compiled and edited by the Brahma
Kumaris Information Services in association with The
Brahma Kumaris World Spiritual University (U.K.),
registered charity No. 269971. Any profit derived from the
sale of these books has been covenanted to the
BKWSU (UK) to further its charitable activities.

Contents

INTRODUCTION

Some books have a personality of their own - each page seeming to speak to your heart, as well as your head. This is one of those books. A bedside companion that provides pointers for dreams... a guide to illuminate dim patches in our lives... an inner voice that gently sways the soul on its meditation journey... or even a watchful prompt, reminding us to remember the journey's destination.

In 'The Setting, Rowing Out, Preparing, and Invoking', Anthea Church sets the scene of the meditation journey, allowing us to follow at our own pace. Then, firstly finding God as 'The Beautiful One', we are led to explore a series of images that challenge and stimulate our notions of God's love and knowingness. Have you ever thought of God as your 'Psychiatrist'? Or 'Power House'? Or as the 'One Who Gets Things Done'? These are a few of the more surprising relationships that begin to germinate in response to these soul reflections.

Exploring human relationships engages our attention for a whole lifetime, through family, social or work situations. Add to that the exploration of relating to God the soul who can fulfil all relationships, and you get an inkling of the possibilities an individual is capable of experiencing. So, choosing what to hold on to, what to seek in relationships, is surely the key to contentment. Here, Anthea, in her own lyrical style, reveals how she connects with God, what draws her to spend time building on this relationship through meditation, and how this tempers her whole perception of the game of life.

Once you've familiarised yourself with the intent of this little book, leaf through it for inspiration, for directness, for the extraordinary, for comfort. You'll find yourself becoming 'someone with whom God plays'...

Invocation

I know that God does not have a body, that He does not suffer, that He is detached from human folly and excellence. I know that He is a benefactor, but is as tied to the strings of destiny as we are. He cannot interrupt our descent and rescue us, unless permitted by the script, and the script He cannot re-write. I know that while we are souls filled with the scars and sweetness of experience, together with a few unaffected distinctions, He is all distinction. He is peace, purity, wisdom, light. We walk along and hit upon those in moments of crisis or joy; expand suddenly into pure feeling but equally can go the other way. Our beings are anchored by our senses; joy emerges if we see, touch, hear something. If a horror is placed in front of us we retract into fear. God has no senses, so He is not a responder, a partner. He does not wait to come into being, He always is.

But I have the feeling that to make that 'being' accessible, He needs minds upon which to play: still, quiet receptacles into which He can place His peace and have it seen. Jesus was that; Buddha, Moses. But not only them. I think secretly hiding in ordinary places and contexts there are other people who can do it. They may not be flag-flying celebrities, but in their quiet ways you can see God playing.

When God plays with you, the knowledge I have described ceases to be theory, it becomes experience. The peace which you either resist describing because it 'passes all understanding' or you define academically as a detachment from the physical, becomes a feeling, a personal treasure.

I would like to be someone with whom God plays. Privately, quietly in a corner somewhere. Partly because I am inexplicably drawn to that pleasure and partly because I cannot see anything that is of greater value. There are small comforts. There is friendship, community, professional excellence, food, drink, fresh air - there is laughter and oddity, the rare seascape that lifts your soul or the smell of an early morning, overlooking a river. But these are short-lived pleasures and they are also shadowed by the worry that soon they - or I - may be gone. They are perishable and I want something that will last even through death.

I am young still, but I want to prepare. Why should

death storm in, crash through my house and show me in one jubilant second the fragility of my treasure?

I write this to anchor the eternal in my mind, to breathe life into the words I have heard and spoken already, to make of them a subtle existence that hangs peacefully, like the lining in a coat, inside my physical life.

So I have taken a selection of words that I have heard and read in my study; flagged them down, stepped inside them like a driver into a car and felt their particular workings. I know there is danger in this pursuit, that I might cloud with my desire the reality; that touching momentarily the coolness of God, I may fill it with warmth out of fear of His totality, His cold truth. But I take that risk as well as the risk of enjoying language as an end rather than a means. I owe it to myself, to God and to those people who have given so much more than I ever could, in making these teachings public. They sit all day crunched over computers: typing, signing agreements for houses, checking that the colour and number of chairs in our meditation centre are right. They want to be silent and explore the depths of what they know, but they have put that aside for the physical obligations that having a truth involves.

I have not done that. I am free to come and go as I wish, like a lay Buddhist who brings food and drink to the shaven monks. I would like to use that freedom wisely.

The Setting

Secluded place at the

foot of the ocean: an

image of my mind.

Many times meditating, I have seen a small house in a place where you wouldn't expect to see a house. It is nestled in rocks and so you miss it if you do not look carefully. This house is real. It exists in the harbour at Dartmouth, Devon. When I was small we used to go for boating picnics and I loved the moment when we passed from the river into the sea. This house, too tiny to be lived in, marked that line. It stood underneath Dartmouth castle; looked like its child.

It is not real to me any more. I have not seen it for years but it has become for me an image of how I would like my mind to be: a secluded place at the foot of the ocean. A place in which unseen exploration can go on and be experienced as a holiday, a break from routine. I row out to this quiet place from time to time and take up where I left off. If I was looking at how visions work, I would go back to that. Obligations, personal shortcomings, laziness even, called me away, but when I come back, my understanding is where I left it - undisturbed.

I want to spend more time in that house now - to go to it again and again and think about God. I want to turn His eyes so that in His looking, I will see the secrets that lie behind that which, without love, is mere information.

Rowing Out

Loved, it acts as a

magnet to pull me

to itself. My clear,

quiet nook.

I have a few moments. Not many but enough to make that inward trip. Before, picnics involved a whole day and so much organizing. We were children and the planning was as good as the outing itself. I keep the lightness of childhood with me, the easy joy and quickness to forgive, but I use what I have learned as an adult: to pack up fast, to row away from routine without too much fuss.

I am propelled by keeping the shape of my nook clear. Loved, it acts as a magnet to pull me to itself. There is not much effort involved. Only sometimes, when I haven't visited for a while, is there a coldness between us.

Then I have to flex the muscles of my mind, think hard, like a person cutting away undergrowth to make a path. The world's claims and self-made distractions grow as fast as weeds. I must be attentive to that.

Preparing

Reaching, touching inner space,

I join each room with a single

mood: peace.

I move around this inner space that
I have reached, touching it. I am
like someone smoothing the bottom
sheet of a bed before lying on it.
Nothing can happen in here unless
I have glanced over it, joined each
room with a single mood: peace.
That is the starting point.

Invoking

Guiding my solitude

into a shape that

will later contain

him.

I have my thoughts ready. I place them side by side on the table before me like cards I will later read carefully, slowly, individually. I put them in an order. I want to get through them in a month, turn each into an experience upon which God will look with love. They say if you think about someone a lot, you eventually see them. I'd like to see God and feel the different fragrance of each form He has, spreading into this space of my mind.

I start with His names and I address Him directly as if He were here with me, guiding my solitude into a shape that will later contain Him.

The Beautiful One

You are so various;

so full of surprises.

Absolute; still; pure.

You are beautiful to me because you are pure. I go on and on thinking about you and I come only to more purity. There is no stopping point, no disappointment, you are utter.

You are beautiful because you do not compromise your truth to console me. You tell me I am a sinner if it is true. Humans forgive me too easily.

You are beautiful because your absoluteness creates in me a longing to please you and that longing is not subservience but self-improvement.

You are beautiful because your qualities have not grown out of experience. They are not the sweetness that follows pain bravely born, they are there because they are there: still, unchanged strengths.

And each one is separate and distinct. Your peace is different from your purity. Your role as judge is distinct from the warmth of your mothering. There are endless opportunities in the thinking of you. Like a face that, changing by the second, is a pleasure to watch. You are so varied; so full of surprises.

Lord of the Poor

Acquisitiveness shuts
you out. The wind
can sing when the
tree is bare

Yes you are beautiful because you are so rich. You know everything, but your affections go most easily to those who have nothing.

Your loving gaze does not stop on the struggling academic as much as upon the old Indian mataji rolling her chapattis. You love her simplicity and the way poverty makes her so careful with what she has.

You light up at honest efforts and uncelebrated conquests, little victories experienced in corners.

You are not pleased with me when I cushion myself with possessions, with public applause or insult. My acquisitiveness shuts you out.

I want to put everything down now, once and for all - desire and unfulfilled desire - and be like a bare tree through which the wind can be heard.

I have enjoyed life but I want to die now gracefully, while I am still alive. Then maybe you will visit me. And you will like my emptied spirit. I would like you to feel comfortable that way with me.

The Power House

Unflinching,

uninfluenced,

eternal

strength

changes me

forever.

I knew your presence would not just be a quietness, it would be a whirlwind. I am a little afraid of that; you may dismantle my thoughts, wipe everything away with your touch and make me start again.

There were people in my life who could do that. With a single word, they destroyed my hopes and remade them differently. Looking back, I am grateful to them because they changed me for a while.

Your power changes me forever. It knocks whole walls down, even washes my house away completely. But I trust you and need to know that you are capable of such dynamism.

It excites me to think of you as a thunderbolt, and all the more because I know that just as quickly you will become gentle and involve yourself in my destiny.

I would like to be resilient enough to take you, to make myself a tiny replica of your strength: unflinching, uninfluenced, eternal.

My
Psychiatrist

You do not need

my weakness to

make you strong.

I trust your

piercing look.

You are an impersonal force that moves through us like a storm, but you are also intricately involved. Many people have tried deconstructing me. In subtle ways, when they looked into my eyes, I could see they were trying to find the inconsistency. Maybe I have done it myself. If so, I am sorry, because it is a sin.

When you look at me in that piercing way, I am happy because your perfection makes you a safe doctor. You do not need my weakness to make you strong.

I should like you to sit here in front of me and dig up my mind completely, bring to its surface the worst atrocity and the greatest strength and make of that combination what you will.

I trust myself with you because you know of my past and my future and you can see without reacting to the contrasts inside me as they are.

Social Worker

I do not see you
crowded. You find
a means of giving
through others.

When I think of you as this, I wonder if I can accommodate people's needs as generously as you do. I prefer your quiet self to you the benefactor.

But this thought does not last long, for I know you have a way of serving people that brings them to the quietness that is intrinsic to your own being.

You must be sent so many messages, so many pleas, but when I think of you I do not see you crowded because you have a way of giving just the right thing and so satisfying people without a song and dance. You find a means to give that makes the gift unrecognisable as yours. It comes through another person's eyes or the casual reassurance of their words. And then you slip away.

I like it that you cannot be seen. And I like it that those gifts do not offer soft consolation or encourage liberalism. They set a fire alight inside that makes one want to sacrifice everything.

If you were a person, people may not like your toughness. That makes me like you more.

The
Creator

Patient, to see

beyond all the

mess; piecing

together

perfection.

You seem to be piecing together a huge construction. Fetching materials from all over the place and fitting them together. I am outraged sometimes at the combinations you create. It doesn't always feel right at the time, but you have a special way of seeing how a temporary connection between people, places, scenes will lead to a small beauty. The people will fall away from each other and something will be left between them that is vital for the future.

I find you remarkably patient: to see beyond all that clutter and mess to the nugget of gold behind it. I like to keep everything I have made, but you know all about discarding what is not absolutely right.

I wrote a calligraphed letter once to the Pope. It was in Polish and it took three days to complete. When I had finished I knew that there was one flaw in it. I decided to ignore it; no one would notice. Then someone walked past it with wet hair and smudged it. That was an accident but your hand was in it somewhere because you wanted that letter to be perfect.

In calling you, I know I am invoking your perfectionist spirit to work upon me. That is the one adventure I am willing to go on. Otherwise, I'd just like to stay quietly at home.

My
Surgeon

You can
make my
spirit young
again. You
cut away my
prejudice.

I am afraid of surgeons. They do not ask permission for what they do. Their entry is cold. They cannot achieve anything without cutting, and as I rise out of sleep, I say things they shouldn't hear.

Why is it that I do not mind your free access to my soul? What is it about you that makes me feel so safe? I know that what you can do to me is more far-reaching and dramatic than what an ordinary surgeon can do and that it may involve some pain, but I relish it because it cannot fail to lighten me.

You can do what no surgeon can. You can make my spirit young again. You cut away my prejudice so that my responses are fresh and spontaneous.

Sometimes I do not know when you have been until afterwards. I knew there was a slowness, an inwardness to the day but I did not know it was you at work and so I had not the chance to worry or question. It is better when you do not ask.

My Purifier

Not fire or
flood. I prefer to
be cleansed by
you and your
strong laws.

A single thought caught from you in passing is like a storm of rain, washing silt away, moving buildings, changing the landscape, separating people from what they know.

If I have the choice, I would prefer to be cleansed by you and not by flood or fire. Because you do it logically and to a plan. Your thought comes to me and everything wrong that it encounters inside falls away. Water and fire push themselves upon people, indiscriminately.

I know that, in order to be cleansed by you, I must already be clean; must be a bright, spacious house inside which you feel happy to sit. That is the readiness you ask for. And I remember that your coming is a sign that I am fit for your fierceness. If I am too casual, I know that you do not bother. You just think: let life work on her, not Me. And you withdraw.

I like the feel of your intervening thoughts. The feel of your strong laws standing between me and myself. You make me free by the boundaries you set around me; the silent warnings which I once longed for from teachers and friends. You do not destroy my sins but you stand me at a distance from them, so that if I touch, I am shocked. To touch is to be impure.

My Judge

I will watch your

eyes and urge them

to signal frailties.

Now, not later.

As judge, I would like you to come to me now. Do not wait until the end. I hate the thought of a dreary procession in front of you like an army inspection. I would rather you told me about my unpolished boots now.

I know that means checking myself in advance. Though I like our casual relationship, the catching of an eye, the joke or whispered insight, I know that in order to avoid your stern face later, I must also jump to attention and accept the fact that formality is also a part of you.

I think I have been frightened by conformity in the past and have misinterpreted sameness as obedience. I hope that you will judge me not on this, but on the purity of my heart. I am willing to work on it, so that if you were to visit my cottage, you could search it for nastiness and find none: no jealousy in a corner or lust for power, but a calmly bare room from which you could do your work. So I will watch your eyes from now on and urge them to signal frailties I have not noticed. Small shocks I can take, but not the sudden knowledge of failure when it is too late to retake the exam.

My Guide

I love the fact you lack

charm in this role. You

just intervene, sharply.

With you as my guide, I feel I could navigate very rough waters. That listening to your whispered direction, I could get through anything. Your advice is so intelligent and quick. You do not ramble or boss but place a single suggestion amidst the muddle and it makes a pathway through.

I love the fact that you measure your words. You know the journey is dangerous and there is not time to chat about everyday occurrences when the possibility of falling is so great. You know what I often forget, that a single thought can cause damage and a single thought save.

I love the fact that you lack charm in this role. You just intervene, sharply, like a stick tapping dancing legs that are slacking.

I love moving in your company, because then my day is a series of light, easy steps. Without you I walk much further and get nowhere. Or else I get to my perceived destination (tasks done, work completed) and forget the destination that you have fixed for me. You keep my mind deep, cut the thread that ties it to the senses, and release it into a bigger, more interesting world.

I think that if you were with me, I could cross even the most dangerous border safely, and on the other side there would be heaven. You are unromantic in your strictness, but you have kept my belief in heaven firm.

Bestower
of
Fortune

Small, invisible
miracles fill each
scene with peace and
adventure.

I remember when I was a child there were some people whose presence made me feel that everything would turn out well. They brought safety and luck. When they were there everyone relaxed, sure of their own success. Your presence is like that. You place a gift in each scene, which makes it magical. You just have to be there and events happen which fill me with happiness: small, invisible miracles. And the difference between you and my lucky people is that, simply by thinking of you, you are there. They need buses, trains, a reason to come. I must remember this: that if I am open to the opportunities of each scene, you will be there. You enter the opportunity rather than the scene itself, as love is felt between the words.

And I have noticed that you are especially ready with gifts when the situation is unforeseen. Sudden work comes, which I had not wanted, and you watch to see if I am aware of the chances it offers.

My invocation here involves action. I must not just sit in my small house dreaming, hoping my quietness will draw you. I must go out and act. You like adventure as well as peace.

Bestower
of
Wisdom

Master of timing, you

bestow respect for time and

each one's rhythm.

In this, you are the master of timing. You know how to wait until the exact right moment and then you watch us blossom. I, in contrast, want to fill my inner house with treasure because I am excited by it, but you let things be for a while, let them settle and strengthen. Then you come.

Your presence in this role is as a gentle hand upon my shoulder steadying my enthusiasm. I want to run and jump towards you but you make me walk because you know my speed can be hurtful to those on my path. Some days, I know you just wish me to be still. You have given me a deadline and yet your wisdom sees the value in a breathing space.

God, you have such faith in last minute completions. You will not let me get there in advance and feel safe, you will get me there only just in time and in the "only just" is your enjoyment.

You do not hurry nor do you touch. If something is going wrong, you just watch. I would want to interfere. But interferers stop people learning.

It is not information you bestow then, not even knowledge quite, but a respect for time and each person's different rhythm. Your presence as the wise one calms my thumping heart.

The
One
who
gives
Visions

To make something so
beautiful it would
change someone. This
key is yours.

You have told us that only you hold the key to visions. What is behind that door which you hold locked? An image bank, a subtle cinema; what is it? More than to receive a vision, I would like to enter that room with you and participate in your despatch. To arrange the slides or select the recipients. To superimpose one image upon another, to make something so beautiful that it would change someone. Better, I would love you to use a room of my house for this task: a dark room for developing pictures to send to people.

I have a feeling that this part of your work is deeply personal. Maybe it is the private pleasure you keep for quiet moments between your other obligations, like a hobby, a sport. Maybe doing this gives you the same feeling as spinning cotton gave Gandhi, the activity he returned to in the peace of his evening verandah after too much publicity.

I should like to be one of your family, like Gandhi's wife, and watch you as you do this. If I could not participate, I could promise quietness and an appreciation of the pictures you make.

The One who can See the Future

The future laid out
before you is the
source of your
stillness, goodness...

Thank God for someone who knows how it will all turn out. The rootedness of that makes me feel strong like a tree under which new lovers come and go everyday.

It is the source of your stillness, this knowledge. We move from past to present, present to future as if it were all new, but you have the future already set out before you, so in a sense you don't have to do anything. When I close my eyes and meet you in this form, I invoke a stability, a resistance to shock which I need, as my wings grow lighter and more refined. You are so refined we cannot even see you, and yet you are utterly solid, unshakeable.

I should like my small house to have that same combination of delicateness and brute strength. So that even if the sea swallowed it, it would go down intact - dignified and quiet - and rest on the seabed until it was safe to surface again.

Existence is truly a completely different thing for you. There are no memories, blocks, dreams. You are one solid line of goodness that cannot be broken by even the most awful of human atrocities. You see all our changes but you stay the same. I marvel at that.

Master of Three Worlds

Free, total Spirit,

yours is the art of

living tuned at all

levels.

I know people who are very spiritual and those who are practical and well earthed. They need each other to stay steady and balanced.

You are the only being I can think of who has the art of living at all levels so tuned. You don't have a body, but you know how one works as finely as if you had lived in one for years. You aren't an angel or a poet but you understand the world of imagery and subtle gestures. And as total spirit, free of ties, you are the perfect master of the highest world, which is just silence.

More than all of that is the skill with which you move between all three. You are not shocked by the tumult of matter nor do you feel naked in silence. In seconds you can go from one to the other, like someone dying and being born again a different sex and colour with no gestation time. I should like that speed and bravery, to stop this gradual growing into spirituality and to be able to go in a second to a different state of mind. Then be still within it without looking back or wondering if something is left behind.

For that you will need to make my inner house into a tardis, a time machine. Not a cosy, rooted place but a light container that can move at will. In preparation for that, I shall wipe its interior clean of ornament or sentimentality. Nothing of the past.

The One who changes Thorns into Flowers

I must call you

at even the trace

of a thorn. You

soften the heart.

You soften people. I know that because I have watched people who are close to you do the same. I have watched resentment disappear from faces, and peace take its place. And I too have felt your presence melt my bad feelings into a flood of ease and acceptance.

I want to keep you in this form on the line between my kindness and my cruelty. To be able at a second's thought to call you to dispel a nastiness and open my heart again. Nastiness hurts the giver as much as the receiver - more - but sometimes the love that follows it is stronger; one wants so much to compensate that one's gestures are large and expressive. But a beautiful life is one free of those contrasts as a sea is beautiful when unbroken by rock or a morning landscape by people. I must call you earlier, at the very inception of nastiness, before it has had time to find a form in thought.

To keep you close, I know I must accept my own capacity to hurt, to move the wrong way. If I forget that, I cannot find you until it is too late and I have spoken. Honesty is what attracts you in this form, and the knowledge that your part is played on that uneven stage between my unkindness and perfection.

Alchemist

Truth is what makes you
gold. I would like to be
your apprentice in this.

When I read too many books or stay too long with people who question, I can feel my mind solidifying into a form that cannot travel into subtlety.

As alchemist, I call you in the quiet of the morning to shift my mind and make it into a fluid shine. But now I'd like to feel you not just in the morning but between the pages of the books I read, the words of the adults I mix with so that I stay golden all the time.

At the moment when the shine is dulling, I shall turn to you and briefly absent myself from my surroundings to catch your eye and see the truth, because truth is what makes you gold. Stone is so unhopeful. And, since you are eternally golden, will you turn me also into an alchemist, a person who polishes the minds of other people? I should like to be your apprentice in this.

The One who Sings the Song of Knowledge

There are the words,
and there is the music
within them: sweet,
heart language.

Invocations

I love music. I love the way it can enter my being directly and uplift it. It bypasses my intellect and reaches my heart in a language I do not fully understand.

Your music is knowledge, and it too has a private language that hides inside the words the ears hear. Yes, there are the words and there is the music inside them: that subtle sweetness that can change one's mood completely.

In this inner house I should like there to be a small corner where you feel happy to play your music and where, sitting with you peacefully, I can catch the secrets that are hidden in your personality.

When I feel a secret touching my mind, it is like hearing a sound so quiet and beautiful that you'd miss it if you weren't alert. That sound grows, however, and lasts, while ordinary music fades. It grows and lasts and solidifies into a piece of treasure that I store in a corner of myself. The more I store your treasure, the more I feel you will come to me, for you will feel that you are entering a place that is of yourself.

My
Servant

Humble, I show

you my needs.

Humble, you fill

the gaps in my

spirit.

You serve me when I am honest about my needs. When I tell someone, whom in your wisdom you have placed above me, which quality it is that I lack, you bring it to me directly. I shut you out when I do not admit that I need anything, am too proud to own up to my failures. As you are humble in serving me, I must be humble in expressing my dependence on you.

For you to be my servant, I have to risk my reputation and say squarely where I stand. But not in public, not to anyone - just to that particular person whom you have appointed. I need faith, then, as well as honesty, that in telling them, I am telling you. They have won that position because of their transparency, their ability to reflect you as you are, at the moment of my asking.

You fill in the gaps in my spirit so quietly, as though I had done it myself. And so that when the problem next occurs, your hand is upon it, gently edging it to the side to make room for the virtue that I lack. To have you as servant, I declare openly my shortcoming and you respond to it in such a concealed way that I hardly notice.

There needs to be other people admitted into my inner house if I want you as my servant.

Lord
of the
Tree

Seed of all things,

You place our strength

where it will flow to

branch, twig and leaf.

You are the seed of all things and so you can see where the power lies and whose mind is worth touching. I have noticed that when there is a task to be done, you do not go to everyone equally with your inspiration, but you go to one and make that one the leader, even if that leadership is unspoken. You know that democracy does not work, that every flower has a root, that at the end of branches is a brittle weakness. We are not equal. So you put your strength where the strength already is. And then that strength is passed on - branch to twig to leaf.

To experience you as Lord in this way, I have to renounce the pleasures that make me peripheral: to move in and away from the senses, the foliage and the flowers - life's obvious gifts - and love barely, by the root. I have to want nothing that can come to me from outside and everything that comes from you, inside.

The One who gets Things Done

To be with just you -

that's my effort; in each

task, to feel your presence.

This morning I did a lot in a short time. Yesterday I did a little in a long time. Why? Was it just a matter of enthusiasm and energy and the right amount of sleep? Was it just the state of my body and the willingness of my mind to focus?

Yes, mainly. But there is more to it than that. When you consider the task worthy, your power is behind it and then I feel that you have done it. If you do not, I am doing it on my own and that is dangerous.

My way to you as God, the one who gets tasks done, is to consult you before I begin. To judge, in looking at your face, whether or not I am embarking on a worthwhile venture. And, if a shadow of a doubt comes between us to block out your presence, then maybe I should stop.

For me to feel you in this form I need to give up ownership of everything I do. To make each task an empty container into which you can place the power or the people to get it done, or the direction not to do it at all.

I must not fill anything in life with feeling other than my effort to be with you. Unlike most other things, that can never be wrong.

My Liberator

I'll bring myself to you,

for changing. Eye to eye,

revealing treasure.

When I look into your eyes, you liberate me. I can feel the problems that make life tighten around me like a straight jacket, loosening and reducing until they are small enough to enter you and be taken. Eye to eye, you free me so that one moment I am caught and the next I can fly.

For this, I have to draw a line around a situation and contain it. Not let it spill into my whole life, but make of it a prohibited place. It is easier for you to lift away something I have not touched too much. If I think about it, I make it too heavy to carry upwards into your eyes.

So, in my inner house, I shall make a special room in which to place the parts of life I find hard. I shall not invite you into that room, for that would be like inviting royalty into the garden shed. Instead, when you are there, I'll bring to you a part of myself that I have stored there and watch you not just take it, but turn it into a treasure.

I shall give it to your eyes and you will return it, changed.

Jeweller

Sorting us through your

fingers: soul jewels of

precious, peculiar beauty.

Every soul is a jewel and every soul who thinks of you a lot is a special jewel. I think you must immensely enjoy seeing us as jewels, sorting us through your fingers and setting us in places that would best become our colour and form.

And when I think of you doing this, I want to join you: watch each person carefully and see their individual and peculiar beauty. Their essence. Once that has happened, the person is in some way one's own because one has seen them clearly.

You do not see the straw - the superfluity - that surrounds each one of us. You do not even finger it but come to us direct, knowing our strength. To join you in your sorting, I have to disregard the straw as well and go straight to the jewel inside.

And when I cannot find the jewel, I remind myself that this is because the value of the stone is such that it needs extra protection. There is something particularly precious wherever there is straw.

The Destroyer of my Obstacles

When I thank it, then you

join me and our strong,

double voice leaves just light.

An obstacle is a blessing. It slows me down and makes me more considerate. If there were no obstacles, there would be no caution. So my first thought when one comes is to thank it. When I thank it, you can participate in its transformation. I notice you do not come when I am resentful. You pay attention, but your heart isn't in it. Sometimes I have even seen you look away.

Thanking makes me stop and look carefully at what it is that has come and why. And when I see the significance of it, only then do I begin to feel your company flooding into my heart and bringing hope.

You repeat and strengthen the thoughts I am already having, like a strong voice joining a small, piping one. Until I am absolutely sure that my perception has been right. That strong, double voice penetrates the obstacle, for it is like a body that has a soul. And our joint, repeated focus on the soul of the obstacle makes the bulk of it fall away until there is only light left.

The Magician

My mind, heart,

face and eyes slip,

unafraid, into yours

for a moment.

Your presence makes magic happen. What was hard evaporates into a pleasure; what was a carelessness on my part suddenly becomes a point of attention. You change the furniture in my mind so that my house looks different.

To invoke you, I must face you as I am. Not quickly rearrange myself to be presentable, but look with that lovely feeling of openness that is a giving of oneself entirely; a child's way. Yes, I am a child before you, who has not yet learned possessiveness. You can touch what you like and change it. My looking at you in this way is a surrender of my own features. My mind and heart, my face and eyes slip unafraid into yours for a moment and re-emerge changed.

If I have not given myself to anyone else, then you come to me. Otherwise I am a mind already fingered and you will not touch. And what is most beautiful about you in this role is that you work in secret. Sometimes even I do not know what you have done to me until it has happened; so complete are you that you do not need an entourage or publicity to announce your work. The purer I am, the more quietly you can do your task.

Gardener

In the garden of my soul,

sow your bright, secret,

early morning seeds.

One thing I find very beautiful about you is that only flowers grow in your garden. There are no weeds. Your mind produces slow, careful thoughts that open out into bright, single colours, so that when they are spoken they are remembered. In our garden these thoughts are numbered because all around them are the fast, casual thoughts that are like weeds.

So I call you in the early morning when my mind has nothing to respond to. I am a bare patch in which you can sow your seeds. In the daytime I am so busy responding, that to touch me would be like trying to hold a horse that is moving at a gallop.

Those seeds that you place are so precious because they turn into the laws by which I live my life. Flowers yes, but also the gentle borders within which I take my steps. Without them, I move without boundaries and that is dangerous. The seeds are also secrets. They will not manifest immediately, but will grow slowly like trees. They are the foundation of the future. To hear those thoughts I have to look into your eyes at night and let you lift from my mind the burden of the day. Then in the morning I am ready for you.

The
Businessman

*Your love is
unconditional; your
giving is not: you
own my heart.*

I like your toughness. I like the fact that, though your love is unconditional, your giving is not. You expect a return. But that is also a part of your giving because my return is my own self - improvement. And I want that as much as you.

You give where there won't be any wastage, like a person investing money in a safe place. So to have you do business with me, I must make my house safe. Safe means pure. Pure means no casual visitors from outside. To be friendly, yes, but to admit anyone into my heart, no. Only you can have ownership of my heart, and I have noticed that you watch me carefully to see whether I am worth your proprietorship.

Once you have made that decision, it is you who brings people to visit, and I have to keep remembering that it is not I who have chosen who comes in and who does not. I remind myself daily that you are managing me, making fruitful the existing factors in my life (my friends, family, job) and creating new ones that I had never dreamed of. I worry when I think it is I who have to make all the decisions. I begin then to look like an adult with a mortgage and too much responsibility. You want me to be a child.

My Innocent Lord

Carefulness. And there
you are, freely tipping
treasure into my mind!

I feel you most powerfully as the innocent Lord in the morning time in India. In the quiet of the mountains, it is as though you are at ease tipping treasure into my mind. Not as the gardener, with circumspection - a seed here, a seed there - but wildly, freely with no reserve.

I get up from half an hour of remembering you and I am rich. When I sat down, I was ordinary. Why is it there that I feel your innocence most? Because of the atmosphere, the white, stone walls, the carefulness of the people?

Everything they do, down to the way they hang a towel on a hook to dry, they do by a system. And somehow, because of that, you feel free to dance. You are like a celebrity only willing to perform under the right conditions. Your passion and brilliance is safe when it is contained within fastidiousness.

To dance with you as freely as that all the time, I must domesticate myself: sit straight, dress right, keep my house in order. I used to think those were petty concerns. Now I know they are part of invocation.

My Boatman

You ride the rough;

in the calm you are

quiet. You teach the

way of the water.

You can do nothing about the water but you can steer the boat through it. When the water is rough, I remember you are there and enjoy the spectacle of your skilful navigation. As boatman, you are so calm and so clever. When a rough wave comes you ride it. When it is calm you are quiet. You know what I keep forgetting - that the water will never be the same, that it is water's nature to fluctuate. You also know that, come what may, the boat will reach its destination.

I am in trouble when I think I am the boatman as well as the boat. I am happy when I am just the boat: passive, unafraid, because you are at my helm. It is in those moments that I most enjoy the journey you are taking me on.

To keep you with me as boatman I must achieve that odd combination of calmness and excitement. Be ready to be taken into rough water and yet do nothing about it but sit tight and look into your eyes. Your eyes are truthful and that truth penetrates deep into my being. It acts as an anchor which I know even the roughest mental storm cannot dislodge. The roughest storms come when I am deceived by my own mind.

The
Lord
of
Immortality

What visions

you must see!

Each scene a

moving pattern

of qualities...

What visions you must see! You who are not distracted by the small things in life that are to do with the body. With no mouth to feed, no form to clothe, no shelter to find, it is as if your seeing must be simply a moving pattern of qualities. When I see a mountain, what do you see? When I see a tree, what do you see? When I see a face what do you see? I should like to see with your eyes, to see the clear line between love and attraction, the difference between arrogance and intelligence. I should like to see to the depth of a person just as you do, to the heart of a scene as you do.

For that, I travel up and away from this house to which I call you. I find your perspective, your high position and look down on the earth from where you are.

It is like standing on my head. It is easy. And to do it makes me strong because it stops me getting caught in the detail of my own life. This also happens when I see disaster. Mass violence shakes one out of petty intensity.

But I would prefer to sail towards the unlimited than be shocked into it.

The Comforter of Hearts

Miracles!

For we who have travelled

through time - your gentle,

healing touch.

We all need you as this: we who have travelled so far through time and seen so much, need your gentle, unobtrusive touch to heal us. If you visit me as this, I should like everyone I know to be present in the room for I think that if each of us felt that touch just once, we should know how to help people.

I have felt it often in a momentary glance from you. A kind of sweeping away of worry that makes me able to sit down and think clearly how to proceed. It is a touch that unties knots, unclenches fists, relaxes. It is the touch of a mother opening a child's hand so that it puts down a stone it has been grasping too long.

I should like you with me all the time as this, because I believe that miracles would happen if we all put down our tightly held views and accepted each other. If I had to choose any form for you to come in - like a guest choosing an outfit - I would choose this one.

Brahma Kumaris Centres

in the United Kingdom and Ireland

London
Global Co-operation House, 65 Pound Lane,
London NW10 2HH
Tel: 0181 459 1400 Fax: 0181 451 6480

Nuneham Courtenay
Global Retreat Centre, Nuneham Park, Nuneham Courtenay,
Oxon OX44 9PG
Tel: 01865 343 551 Fax: 01865 343 576

Edinburgh
20 Polwarth Crescent, Edinburgh, EH11 1HW
Tel: 0131 229 7220 Fax: 0131 229 7220

Cardiff
8 Haxby Court, Felbridge Close, Atlantic Wharfe,
Cardiff, CF1 5BH Tel: 01222 480 557

Dublin, Ireland
36 Lansdowne Road, Ballsbridge, Dublin 4, Ireland
Tel: (+353) 1 660 3967

Invocations

WORLD HEADQUARTERS
BRAHMA KUMARIS WORLD SPIRITUAL UNIVERSITY
PO BOX NO.2, MOUNT ABU, RAJASTHAN 307501, INDIA

*INTERNATIONAL CO-ORDINATING OFFICE
AND EUROPEAN REGIONAL OFFICE*

Global Co-operation House, 65 Pound Lane, London NW10 2HH, UK
Tel: (+44) 181 459 1400 Fax: (+44) 181 451 6480

REGIONAL OFFICES

AFRICA

PO Box 12349, Maua Close, off Parklands Road,
Nairobi, Kenya
Tel: (+254) 2 743 572 Fax: (+254) 2 743 885

AUSTRALIA AND SOUTH EAST ASIA

78 Alt Street, Ashfield, Sydney NSW 2131 Australia
Tel: (+61) 2 716 7066 Fax: (+61) 2 716 7795

NORTH AND SOUTH AMERICAS

Global Harmony House, 46 S. Middle Neck Road,
Great Neck, NY 11021 USA
Tel: (+1) 516 773 0971 Fax: (+1) 516 773 0976

Your Local Contact is:

OTHER BRAHMA KUMARIS CENTERS

Harmony House, 46 South Middle Neck Rd., Great Neck, NY 11021
Tel: 1-516-773 0974 Fax: 1-516-773 0976

1821 Beacon St., Brookline, Boston, MA 02146
Tel: 1-617-734 1464 Fax: 1-617-734 7263

1609 W. Chase Avenue ,Chicago, Il. 60626
Tel: 1-312-262 2828 Fax: 1-312-262 3605

8009 Hollywood Blvd., Los Angeles, CA 90046
Tel: 1-213-876 5545 Fax: 1-213-876 2587

4160 S.W. 4th Street, Miami, FL 33134
Tel: 1-305-442 2252 Fax: 1-305-442 6745

710 Marquis, San Antonio, TX 78216
Tel: 1-210-344 8343 Fax: 1-210-342 8888

401 Baker Street, San Francisco, CA 94117
Tel: 1-415-563 4459 Fax: 1-415-563 4673

302 Sixteenth Street, Seal Beach, CA 90740
Tel: 1-310-430 4711 Fax: 1-310-430 9754

Mind's Eye Museum, 2207 E. Busch Blvd., Tampa FL 33612
Tel: 1-813-935 0736 Fax: 1-813-985 1591

TRINIDAD
55-57 Pointe-A-Pierre Road, San Fernando
Tel: 1-809-653 3766 Fax: 1-809-658 5304

CANADA
897 College Street, Toronto, Ontario M6H 1A1
Tel: 1-416-537 3034 Fax: 1-416-537 1319

Introductory courses in meditation are offered at each of our centers
throughout the country, free of charge.
For more information, and the address of a center near you,
please contact one of the above centers.